Second Coming on the Johnny Show

a play
by George Arthur Lareau

SUFI GEORGE BOOKS
TUCSON

ROYALTY FREE—PERMISSION NOT NEEDED FOR PRODUCTION

ISBN 978-1-885570-26-0

Sufi George Books: http://sgbooks.sufigeorge.net

Table of Contents

PRODUCTION AND SET NOTES

The stage is a TV studio set up for a late night talk show. No curtain is used, except for a backdrop curtain at stage right, in front of which the monologues are given. At least one TV monitor is located to one side of the stage, high enough to be easily viewed by the audience.

The set includes a sofa for guests, next to the desk at which the show host sits. Live microphones pick up the monologues, the guest, and the host, so that they are able to speak in normal tones of voice; the theatre is amply equipped with speakers so the audience can hear normal speech levels from the stage.

Large mock-ups of studio TV cameras are located at each side of the stage and, if practical, in the center aisle. One houses a small video camera (such as a home video camera) that feeds the TV monitor, and which is operated during all action by Crewman Five.

At side stage in view of the audience, an engineer operates equipment which switches the TV monitor back and forth between the live TV camera and videotaped titles and commercials, which have been prepared in advance by the theatre company.

Theatre patrons are not admitted to the theatre prior to 15 minutes before performance time. The script allows for a variety of stage business for this 15-minute period. As patrons enter the theatre, the stage is brightly lit, house lights are up full, and the stage manager and crew are visible preparing for air time.

This production does not "begin;"' rather, the audience becomes a part of it when they enter the theatre. The production does not pause nor end until the patrons have left the theatre. It is important that the audience feel they have walked in on an ongoing activity, which continues after they leave. It is also important that the audience feel that they are actually a part of a TV studio audience, at least from time to time. House lights ought not be brought down below medium intensity; the audience should not be separated from the stage by the traditional sharp contrast in lighting. The audience participates in this production.
An applause sign is clearly visible and flashes on and off during the performance to signal for applause.

Seating is reserved, in order to control placement of the audience extras so that they are evenly distributed throughout the house.

During Johnny's monologues, a player flashes over-sized cue cards, which Johnny glances at.

The TV spots to be shown during breaks can be requested from a local TV station. TV spots from advertisers lend an air of reality.

Title cards can be hand-lettered and will be used to introduce the show after each commercial break. There is no curtain call. Each cast member can be videotaped with a credit line, or a more elaborate curtain call production can be made, which can be shown on the studio monitor after the "broadcast" ends.

THE CAST

JOHNNY
Johnny is modeled after Johnny Carson of the Tonight Show

JESUS
A sober-looking middle-aged man, bearded, but not especially remarkable in appearance, voice or otherwise

EDDIE
Eddie is modeled after Ed McMahon of the Tonight Show.

STAGE MANAGER

FIVE STAGE CREWMEN
(The Fifth operates a live camera)

AUDIENCE EXTRAS
(Sprinkled throughout the audience)

BERNIE
The sound engineer

PASSERS-BY
A couple

BILLY BOB JACKSON
A Southern Bible-belt preacher

ALICIA MONROE
A guest on the program

Scene 1, The Pre-Show Set-Up

[This scene may be lengthened with stage business which is in character with the action and dialogue described.]

[Fifteen minutes before curtain time, the stage crew begins its work, as the audience is permitted to begin entering the theatre.]

CREWMAN ONE:
[Lays cable from live camera around stage props to engineer's booth.]

CREWMAN TWO:
[Drags a vacuum cleaner on stage to vacuum sofa, removing cushions first, vacuums sofa, proceeds to vacuum the cushions as he replaces them.]

CREWMAN THREE:
[Hangs microphone over guest spot at end of sofa, using step-ladder.]

CREWMAN FOUR:
[Holds step-ladder to steady it.]

CREWMAN ONE:
[During the above action, brings out a desk mike for host, lays cable out.] [To CREWMAN TWO:] Ain't you done that yet?

CREWMAN TWO:

Hey, I'm paid by the hour!

CREWMAN ONE:
[Can't hear over the vacuum cleaner.] What?

CREWMAN TWO:
[Shouting.] I said, I'm paid by the fucking hour!

CREWMAN ONE:
[Shouting.] Yeah, well we ain't got no fucking hour! We're on the air in about ten minutes!

CREWMAN TWO:
[Looks at sofa.] A..a..ah, that's good enough anyway. [Turns off vacuum, replaces leftmost cushion without having cleaned it. Drags vacuum noisily off stage.]

CREWMAN THREE:
[Moves ladder so he can position monologue microphone in front of curtain backdrop; when he hangs the mike, he leaves the end of the cord hanging in front of the curtain.]

CREWMAN FOUR:
[Goes off stage to get the microphone and cord; returns with it, hands to CREWMAN THREE, steadies his ladder while it is positioned.]

CREWMAN FIVE:
[Goes to live camera, focuses on various spots on the set; the monitor is not turned on, but he seems unaware of this.]

OTHER CREW:
[They place props including ash-tray stand, cup and pitcher of water, coffee table, vase of flowers, several pencils, etc., in appropriate places on set. They carry clip-boards, and check off these items as they are placed.]

10

[It is now curtain time, the announced time of the performance.]

STAGE MANAGER:
[Goes to center stage, clip-board in hand.] Okay, ten-minute check! Let's get this over with! [CREW assembles on stage. CREW take positions as operators of camera mock-ups.] Video first. Camera one, image?

CREWMAN FIVE:
Image.

STAGE MANAGER:
Monitor hot?

CREWMAN THREE:
Shit! The monitor's dead! You switched on, Bernie?

BERNIE:
I'm switched. You'd better get your ass up there and make sure the switch is on.

CREWMEN THREE AND FOUR:
[Move step-ladder to monitor, and turn it on.]

STAGE MANAGER:
Shit! Who turned that thing off? Why tonight? [The monitor comes on.] Okay, camera two, image?

OTHER CREW:
[At camera two.] Image. [Repeat for each camera if there are more than two.]

STAGE MANAGER:
Okay, audio. Monologue mike. Hey, who the hell left that

11

cord hanging there? That'll pick up on camera! Get it the hell out of sight, will you? Bernie, monologue mike?

BERNIE:
Signal.

STAGE MANAGER:
Desk mike?

BERNIE:
Signal.
STAGE MANAGER:
Guest mike?

BERNIE:
Guest mike is dead.

STAGE MANAGER:
Dead? It was okay last night! What the fuck is going on here tonight? Get that ladder over there and see if some asshole turned that off, too!

CREWMEN THREE AND FOUR:
[Move ladder to guest mike, climb up and turn it on.]

BERNIE:
Guest mike signal.

STAGE MANAGER:
I'm gonna have a piece of somebody's ass for this! Fucking Jesus on the show tonight and half the gear is turned off! Okay, props. Ash tray? [Various CREW who have placed the props each answer "Check."]

STAGE MANAGER:
Cup and pitcher of water? Full cup on Johnny's desk?
Coffee table? Pencils on the desk? Flowers? [Etc.,
according to whatever other props are used.] Okay, let's get
our asses backstage. We got four, five minutes to air time.
[All CREWMEN and STAGE MANAGER go back stage.]

Scene 2, The Pre-Show Monologue

JOHNNY;
[Casually walks out through curtain, is recognized by AUDIENCE EXTRAS who applaud. Applause sign flashes. Faces audience, smiling, looking around, rubbing palms together.] Good evening, folks! I'm Johnny. [Applause light flashes, AUDIENCE EXTRAS applaud and cheer vigorously.] Easy does it, now. We're not on the air yet! [Laughs at his joke.]

How many of you have never been in a live studio audience before? ...Most of you. [Looks off stage.] Why is it they never come back? [To audience.] It's the same thing every night. First-timers. They never come back. Listen, will you be different? Will you all promise me that you'll come back? [Loud cheers and whistles from AUDIENCE EXTRAS.]

You're probably wondering what I'm doing out here, since the show hasn't started yet. Well, I like to come out a little early and say hello, look you over, see what I'm in for. [Laughs.] Technically, this is called the "warm up." Yes, that's right. The warm up. From what little I understand, it's supposed to serve two purposes. ...And I ought to be able to remember at least one of them. [Laughs.]

Okay, here's one. This is where you get your training in how to be a studio audience. You see that applause sign? And now that you've been trained as a studio audience.... [Laughs.] No, really now, folks, when the applause sign lights up, you applaud for all you're worth. Or else. [Laughs.] Or else we'll never let you in here again. [To off stage.] Hey, now we know why they never come back! [Laughs.]

So let's give it a practice run, okay? [To off stage.] Would you light up the applause sign? [Conducts the audience in applause. After the applause:] Weak. [Shakes head, eyes closed.] Pitiful. One more time, now, and keep in mind that there are millions of people watching who want to applaud and they can't, not so I can hear it, anyway. [Laughs.] So make me feel like a big star, and applaud so you sound like millions of people. That's about 100,000 apiece. You got it? Cheers, whistles, the works! [Looks off stage, points to applause sign and nods; it lights up. He conducts the audience in applause; the AUDIENCE EXTRAS let it all out. After applause ends, to off stage:] I think they've got it! On to item number two. This is where I tell you a few jokes that are so funny, you'll laugh at everything else I say for the rest of the evening. [Laughs.] Of course, these couldn't possibly be clean jokes. As long as we're not on the air yet, I can say anything I want to, because there's no FCC breathing down my neck. ...Damn it. ...Turd. ...The President is a hero. [Laughs.] I guess you know who our big guest is tonight.

AUDIENCE EXTRAS:
[A few of the AUDIENCE EXTRAS shout:] Jesus!

JOHNNY:
That's right. His first public appearance. Jesus Christ. I can't believe the publicity this has received, can you? A lot of people are taking this guy seriously. That was a capital "G" on "Guy," just in case. [Laughs.] And when I introduce him later on, you had better applaud like hell, just in case.

[Laughs.]

Don't get me wrong. I think we owe a lot to Jesus. Where would we be today if we couldn't say, "Jesus Christ, give me a break!" [Laughs.] But really, I don't know what to think of this guy. He writes a book while he's in a nut house...

AUDIENCE EXTRAS:
Boo-o-o! Boo-o-o!

JOHNNY:
Crazy farm? [Laughs.] And it's a runaway best seller. Millions of people seem to believe that this guy is really the second coming of Jesus Christ. I like that expression, second coming. They say you never forget your first coming. [Laughs.] This Jesus character is so big...

AUDIENCE EXTRAS:
[One shouts:] How big is he? [All other AUDIENCE EXTRAS then turn to their neighbors and say:] Shit, I missed it! I was waiting for a chance to say that!

JOHNNY:
He's so big that we're devoting the whole show to him. We have with us tonight, in addition to Jesus Christ, a lovely lady, Alicia Monroe. [Looks off stage as if he has been called to.] Okay. It's almost air time. I can tell you're going to be a swell audience tonight. And who knows, this may be a night to remember. So hold on to your seats and I'll be right back. [Points to applause sign, which lights up. Walks behind monologue curtain.]

CREWMAN FOUR:
[At side stage.] Fifteen seconds! Ten seconds! Nine, eight, seven, six, five, four, three. [Two seconds later, video rolls

with EDDIE's voice.]

EDDIE'S VOICE:
It's time for...The Johnny Show! [Applause sign lights up.
AUDIENCE EXTRAS lead applause throughout
performance. Title card on monitor reads "The Johnny
Show."] With your host...Johnny! [Monitor shows still
photo of JOHNNY.] With his side-kick, Eddie! [Monitor
shows still photo of EDDIE.] Special guests tonight
include...Alicia Monroe! And yes, you've been waiting for
it...and tonight is the night...Jesus Christ!

Scene 3, The Live Monologue

JOHNNY:
[Rubs his palms, holds them up to stop applause, lowers them and beckons for more applause, laughs, looks off stage, looks over the audience.] And hello to you, too! [After applause ends.] Let's see, what can I talk about?

AUDIENCE EXTRA:
Look at the cue card!

JOHNNY:
Um-hmm. I haven't talked about my butcher for a while. I switched butchers last month. My old butcher became a vegetarian, and I just didn't trust him after that. [Laughs.] My new butcher, though, he doesn't serve just anybody. This guy actually has a clientele. I walk in and other customers say, "Hi, Johnny!" or "Look, there's Johnny." My butcher says, "Hey, you're not one of my customers." Thought he was going to card me on the spot. [Laughs. Then, seriously:]

Is that what they call it when they ask for your ID to make sure you're old enough to drink? This guy wants to make sure you're old enough to eat meat! [Laughs.]

Did you read about the national spelling bee? Oh, come on. It was a big story. Made all the papers. They added a new twist this year. There was a booby prize for whoever spelled a word the wrongest. That's right, the more letters you got wrong, the better your chance of winning the booby prize. The word was "coffee," and the prize went to the person who spelled it "k a w p h y," every letter wrong. [Laughs.]

You wonder what's going to become of people like that, you know? Well, I've figured it out. It seems that the worse you are at spelling, the better your chances of making it in life as a sign painter. [Laughs.] Big sale on vibators. [Laughs.] Fish sanwich. [Laughs.]

Well, I guess you know we have a big show tonight. There's been so much publicity about our guest's appearance that I would guess we have more people watching this program right now than have ever watched a TV show before. I don't even need good jokes on a night like tonight. You noticed.

Anyway, just in case you've been big-game hunting for the past three years and just got back, let me tell you what you're in for. Three years ago, a man who had spent most of his life in a mental institution wrote a book called Yes, I Am. It's been at the top of the best seller list ever since. And the man claims to be none other than Jesus Christ. No one has seen him. That is, he hasn't made any public appearances. I don't mean that he's invisible or anything like that. He insisted that his first public appearance be on my show. I'm flattered, I think.... [Laughs.]

And he kept putting it off, even though we've invited him several times, but in his words, the time wasn't right yet. In the meantime, millions of people have completely accepted his claim that he is the second coming of Jesus Christ. And we also have Alicia Monroe, who has single-handedly promoted the sale of more copies of Yes, I Am than the publisher has. So my guess is that we have an interesting evening ahead of us. We'll be right back after we make some money. [Applause sign lights up. JOHNNY walks to his seat at desk. He checks out his props. The monitor silently shows commercials being aired.]

JOHNNY:
[Calls to BERNIE.] Hey, where are my pencils? What'll I do with my hands? You know what they say about idle hands-they're the devil's playground. I can't have that, especially not tonight.

BERNIE:
[Calls to STAGE MANAGER:] Hey, you! Johnny needs pencils!

STAGE MANAGER:
I thought you said "check" when I asked pencils! You goddamned fuck-up, get those goddamned pencils out there, and I mean hustle your ass! [CREWMAN rushes out with a handful of pencils, gives them to Johnny.]

JOHNNY:
[Handles a pencil, flips it over his shoulder.] Yeah, these'll do fine! [Laughs.]

EDDIE:
[Walks to the guest seat of the sofa, sits. Passes pleasantries with Johnny, not clearly audible to audience. A few minutes pass, during which nothing seems to be happening, except for commercials rolling on the monitor.]

CREWMAN FOUR:
Fifteen seconds! Ten, nine, eight, seven, six, five four, three.

Scene 4, The Letters

JOHNNY:
[Two seconds later.] We're back. We have a big show
tonight. Not since the days of the Beatles has a guest
appearance been looked forward to so much by so many
people. Yes, it's Jesus Christ night on the Johnny Show.
And it's not just the young people. We've been getting
letters from the whole spectrum of American society. And I
happen to have a few of them here. [Reading a letter.]
"Dear Johnny. I have arthritis. Real bad. I am an old
woman, and I would like to shock one more ear of corn
before I die. Will you ask Jesus to heal just my hands, and
the rest of me if He has time." Signed, Rosemary Potts, St.
Joseph, Illinois.

Well, Rosemary, we all go to pot sooner or later. St.
Joseph. Is there really such a place? Is that where they
make the aspirins? [Goes to next letter.] What do we have
here? "Dear Johnny. I have been saved and sanctified for
13 years, but after reading Yes, I Am, I no longer know
where I stand. Will you please ask Jesus to give his opinion
of salvation and sanctification?" Signed, Luella Sweetmore,
Newark, Arkansas.

Luella, what exactly is sanctification? Salvation I know.
That's Billy Graham and Oral Roberts, right? What you
watch on TV when you've already seen the movie and your
team's not playing. [Laughs.] Does anybody know what
sanctification is?

AUDIENCE EXTRA:
Like a second degree. You can't sin anymore. They have it in the South.

JOHNNY:
It didn't sound like anything we have in California. [Laughs.] Of course, who knows? You can't sin anymore? Does that mean that when you start to sin, you sort of...just freeze? Or that nothing you do can be called a sin? That would be alright, wouldn't it? Woops, I just had lust in my heart. Hey, that's okay, it's not a sin because I've gotten sanctification. [Laughs.] How come Jimmy Carter didn't know about this one? [Laughs.]

AUDIENCE EXTRA:
It's when the Holy Spirit enters you.

JOHNNY:
Okay. I won't argue with that. Let's see what's next here. "Dear Johnny. I haven't read the book, but everybody knows that Jesus has returned. I'm glad he chose your show for His first public appearance. You need it. And that Joan Rivers! She could use a good dose. In Jesus' name, Pearlee Williams, Little Rock, Arkansas."

A good dose of what, Pearlee? Not that you need to get very specific with Joan. She knows what you're talking about whether that's what you're talking about or not. [Laughs.] How many of you people have read the book, Yes, I Am? Amazing. How many of you have read, Yes, I Can by Sammy Davis, Jr.? [Several AUDIENCE EXTRAS hold up their hands.] Well, that's a little better. But I don't understand why I asked that. [Laughs.]
But isn't that odd, here we all are, waiting to meet the man who claims to be the second coming of Jesus Christ...

AUDIENCE EXTRA:
[Shouts:] He is!

JOHNNY:
Have you read the book?

AUDIENCE EXTRA:
Have you read it?

JOHNNY:
What, are you kidding? I'm the guy's host. I'm the guy who has to interview him. What do you think? ...No, I haven't read it, either. [Laughs.] And I try to read all of the best sellers. And talk about best sellers, this is an all-time best seller. But apparently people are buying it and not reading it. I don't understand that.

Anyway, here's another letter. "Dear Johnny, I am a poor man and am afflicted with leprosy. When I lost my hands and feet, I thought my world had ended. But then I discovered the gospel of Jesus and His love, and my life has been filled with heavenly joy ever since the day I gave myself to Jesus. Although God is testing me harshly, I know that heaven awaits me and I am comforted by the love of the Savior. Praise His name! John... [Can't pronounce it.] Mascigluscio, Truth or Consequences, New Mexico."

Leprosy. Ugh. Was it Karl Marx who said that religion is the opiate of the masses? Poor guy needs the strongest stuff he can get. I'd better tell him about sanctification. ...John, if you don't have any hands or feet, how did you write this letter? [Laughs.]

AUDIENCE EXTRA:
Boo-o-o!

JOHNNY:
There was a film on public television about a woman who had no hands and she learned to write with her feet. Did you see that show?

EDDIE:
No, I missed that one.

JOHNNY:
She'd go to the supermarket and write out the check with her foot. No, really. That's some feet, let me tell you. [Laughs.] I wonder if you could learn to write by putting a pencil up your nose? [Tries it.]

AUDIENCE EXTRAS:
Boo-o-o!

JOHNNY:
Snot the most ridiculous thing I ever heard of. [Laughs.] Okay, I admit that was in poor taste. [Flips pencil over shoulder.] Will you forgive me if I say a few pater nostrils? [Laughs.]

Just one more letter. A quickie. "Dear Johnny. I have murdered a man. Will Jesus forgive me? The police don't know." Signed, Leonard March, Route 1, Box 207A, Ames, Iowa. Oh, there's more. "P.S. If you read this on the air, please don't reveal my identity." [Looks at audience deadpan.] Not serious, folks. We wrote that one ourselves. [Laughs.] Eddie, you've got something for us?

EDDIE:
A few of the staff wondered what it would be like if there

26

were a "Dear Jesus" column, you know, like "Dear Abby?" So they came up with a few ideas. Are you ready for this? [Chuckles.]

"Dear Jesus. You are good at explaining the mysteries of life. Can you explain why the splash guards in urinals always splash back?" [To audience.] Now, you ladies may not know what this letter is about.

JOHNNY:
We'd better start with the basics. They've probably never seen a urinal. [To audience.] Ladies, hold your hands up if you have ever been in a men's room.

AUDIENCE EXTRAS:
[A few timidly hold their hands up.]

EDDIE:
A urinal, ladies, is what a man uses in a public rest room when he wants to...well, when he wants to stand up. And they have these plastic splash guards that are supposed to prevent splashing. But it splashes all over anyway. And you can't stand back away from it because then all the gay men will think you are advertising.

JOHNNY:
I always aim to the side of them, myself. Anyway, here's the reply from dear Jesus. "Dear Madder than a wet hen. Think of it as a baptism." [Makes a disgusted face.] Not very good, Eddie, I hope you've got some better ones in here.

EDDIE:
"Dear Jesus. I never believed in you before, but now I do. The reason I never believed in you before is that I have

27

been taking care of my handicapped brother for years. How can God create people who can't lift a hand to help themselves and who laugh all the time? I'm sick of it."

JOHNNY:
"Dear Saddled in Seattle. The weak shall inherit the mirth." If the guy laughs all the time, we could give him a job sitting in the front row. Get to the next one. Hurry.

EDDIE:
"Dear Jesus. I have a weight problem. I have tried dieting, but it only makes me hungry. I am so big that I have to sew my own clothes, and I keep gaining and my clothes pop at the seams. What can I do?"

JOHNNY:
"Dear Big Bertha. As you sew, so shall you rip." [Laughs.] Okay, that one's cute.

EDDIE:
"Dear Jesus. When I pray, nothing happens...

AUDIENCE EXTRA:
We want Jesus!

EDDIE:
"I pray for a lot of things that I never get...

AUDIENCE EXTRAS:
[One chants.] We want Jesus! We want Jesus! [Two others join the chant.] We Want Jesus! [Then all AUDIENCE EXTRAS take up the chant.] WE WANT JESUS! WE WANT JESUS! [All AUDIENCE EXTRAS begin nudging their neighbors, encouraging them to join in the chant.]

28

EDDIE:
"Sometimes I get nice things that I haven't prayed for. [Depending on how long it takes to get chanting going, this speech may be cut short.] So I don't get it, What is it with prayer, anyway?"

CREWMAN FOUR:
[Signals for a break. The gesture is as if holding a bundle of dry spaghetti and breaking it in two toward the floor.]

JOHNNY:
We'll be right back, after this break. [Chanting continues well into break, for as long as AUDIENCE EXTRAS can keep it going. Nothing much happens on stage. Commercials roll on monitor.]

JOHNNY:
[After he gets audience to stop chanting, to audience:] I really do appreciate your enthusiasm, but do want to mention that I'm forced by production considerations to run the show the way it's been laid out. This is television, and the show has to run for two hours, give or take a few commercials, of course! [Laughs.]

So we have to unfold it as it's been planned, or we're in trouble. Jesus will have the full amount of time he requested, so don't think you're going to miss out on a thing. Remember, too, the only people praying, uh, paying for any of this are the sponsors, and we have to do things with that in mind.

But I love your spirit, and keep that up. You're the liveliest audience I've had in months, and I hope you enjoy the show as much as I'm enjoying having you out there. Really, I mean that. Keep up the good work!

CREWMAN FOUR:
Fifteen seconds! Ten, nine, eight, seven, six, five, four,
three.

Scene 5, Alicia

JOHNNY:
We have quite an unusual lady as our first guest tonight,
with some even more unusual stories to tell, I understand.
So let's have a big welcome for...Alicia Monroe!

ALICIA:
[Applause sign lights up. She enters and takes the guest
seat on the sofa.]

JOHNNY:
Alicia, you've probably done more to popularize the book
Yes, I Am than any other person, or institution, for that
matter, including the publisher. Tell us a little about that.

ALICIA:
Thank you, Johnny. First of all, I want to say how honored
I am that you invited me to be on your show.

JOHNNY:
Alicia, everyone is honored to be on my show. What can I
say? [Laughs.] But you're not here by accident, you know.
Our research staff found out about you, and that's why you
were invited. So tell us about it. Earn your plane ticket
from, where is it, Phoenix?

ALICIA:
Yes, your people found me in Phoenix. My home, which I
haven't seen for some time, is Santa Cruz.

JOHNNY:
Oh, so you're a Californian?

ALICIA:
Yes, but that's not very interesting. I mean, there are so
many Californians these days. So anyway, let me tell you
about my experience with the book. It all began about two
and a half years ago. My dear friend Alice Gordon-we
became friends because our names are so similar-Alice and
Alicia...

JOHNNY:
That's a good California reason. [Laughs.]

ALICIA:
Anyway, Alice had multiple sclerosis, you know, MS, and
she saw this book Yes, I Am in a bookstore and on an
impulse-just out of the blue, mind you-she bought it and
took it home, and when she went to bed that night, she was
going to start reading it, but she fell sleep right away and
slept with that book on her, you know, her abdomen, and
when she woke up, she was cured of her MS.

It was a true blue miracle. And she didn't know how it had
happened, but as we talked about it, I was so amazed, I
realized that it had to be that book. So I asked her if I could
borrow it for an experiment. And she agreed, not realizing
what a treasure it was. After all, it was written by Jesus
Christ Himself.

JOHNNY:
So she was really cured? Was that confirmed by a doctor?

ALICIA:
Oh, yes. Her doctor first thought it was a gag, that maybe
she had a healthy twin sister who was posing as her, but he

tested her completely and was completely satisfied that she had somehow been miraculously cured. He even sent a report on it to the medical society.

So anyway, I had this neighbor lady with arthritis, so I told her to try out sleeping with this book on her abdomen. She thought I was nuts, but she did it, and in the morning, you guessed it, no more arthritis.

JOHNNY:
No wonder the book became so popular. What the world needed was another arthritis cure. [Laughs.]

ALICIA:
So it was real clear to me that the Lord was healing through His book, and since I was the only person in the world who knew it, I took up the mission of spreading the word. First, it was the local newspaper, and the next thing I knew, people were writing me letters telling me about their healings from sleeping with this book on their abdomens and enclosing money. Then it was TV and the word really started spreading. In the past three years, there have been well over 100,000 healings, I'm just sure, and people were sending money to me because they didn't know where Jesus was and they wanted to thank somebody. So I used the money to pay for national lecture tours and it's been a heyday for the Jesus book ever since.

JOHNNY:
So people... [Chokes on his laughter.] are you ready for this? So people have been getting healed by touching the hem of his book jacket? [AUDIENCE EXTRAS laugh.]

ALICIA:
[Not laughing.] That's funny, but it's the truth. People don't even have to read it. In fact, I haven't had a chance to read

it yet, myself, I've been so busy.

JOHNNY:
Does this healing power work for everybody?

ALICIA:
I suppose so. I haven't heard of any cases where it's failed.

JOHNNY:
How about yourself? Has the healing power of the book been of any direct benefit to you?

ALICIA:
I've always been as healthy as an ox, as they say. Speaking of which, I understand that at least a few veterinarians have strapped the book to the abdomens of sick animals, with wonderful results. Can you imagine? I haven't heard of any doctors using it, yet, but who knows? The book is gradually putting them all out of business, anyway. Not that I have anything against doctors, which I don't.

JOHNNY:
Tell me a little about your lecture tours. Where do you give your lectures? Churches?

ALICIA:
Churches mostly. A lot of community organizations, too. There have even been instant healings during my lectures. I carry a copy of the book with me and pass it around so people can see what it looks like so they can spot it in the bookstores, and the first thing I know, once in a while, right in the middle of my lecture-I pass the book around at the beginning of my lecture-get it started going around, I mean-and right in the middle of my lecture I'll hear someone shout, "Praise the Lord!" and after the first few times that happened, I knew it meant that someone had

been healed right there on the spot, so I started calling those people up to the front to give a testimonial about their instant healing. But for the most part, it takes the overnight treatment.

JOHNNY:
How do you explain this? I mean, as a matter of pure scientific fact, just how much can happen as a result of sleeping with a book on your belly?

ALICIA:
Johnny, it's not just any book. It's a book that proves that the second coming of Jesus Christ has taken place. They call it faith healing, so I suppose that's part of it, but when it happened to my friend Alice, she didn't know it was going to happen, and even people who don't believe in Jesus the Savior are healed, and while that doesn't seem fair somehow, it does make you wonder if faith is even necessary and if it isn't just the power of the Lord working directly through His book.

After all, some really tremendous power is at work here, and just having faith probably wouldn't be enough of a factor anyway. On the other hand, the healings have certainly brought a lot of new converts to the saving grace of Jesus.

JOHNNY:
That's interesting, Alicia. People have been having their bodies healed, and so they line up to have their souls saved, too?

ALICIA:
It's the power of Jesus at work. He's alive, and in our midst, and the whole country has been waiting for tonight so we can see Him in person and hear His holy words first hand.

CREWMAN FOUR:
[Signals break.]

JOHNNY:
Alicia, that time has just about arrived. We're going to take this break, and when we come back, we'll bring Jesus on right away.

Scene 6, The First Jesus Scene

JOHNNY:
We're back, and without any further ado, let's give a big welcome to...Jesus Christ!

JESUS:
[Comes through curtain, waves at audience modestly, shakes hands with Johnny, takes guest seat on sofa.]

JOHNNY:
So. This is it. Here you are.

JESUS:
You got it.

JOHNNY:
Well, what are you doing here? [Laughs.] I mean, you insisted that your first public appearance be on my show, and I'm flattered, but why was that? The large audience?

JESUS:
Partly that. Principally, though, I knew you would be skeptical of my claim that I am Jesus.

JOHNNY:
You mean, you chose to appear with a skeptic? Why would you do that?

JESUS:
Because, this whole Christianity business has gotten so

totally screwed up that I needed a well-respected skeptic to encourage skepticism.

JOHNNY:
Whoa! You don't want people to believe in you?

JESUS:
Exactly.

JOHNNY:
But in your book, which has stirred quite a sensation, did you say that? Because your book has belief in Jesus at an all time high.

JESUS:
True, millions now believe that I am Jesus Christ come again, and my book played a vital role in accomplishing that. But nothing in the book suggests that people should believe in me.

JOHNNY:
So does that mean that your book is some kind of a trick? That you don't think that you are Jesus, not really?

JESUS:
Oh, I'm Jesus, alright. But believing in Jesus is a bunch of crap.

JOHNNY:
You're saying that believing in you is a bunch of...crap?

JESUS:
I think I already said that.

JOHNNY:
[Laughing at Jesus' remark.] Well, Jesus... I guess I can call you by your first name? Your real name is what, Arnold Mansfield, [looking at book jacket] born in Poughkeepsie.

JESUS:
Whatever you prefer, Johnny.

JOHNNY:
Jesus has a bit more class than...Arnold... [Makes a face...] so let's stick with that. Well, let's get down to it. With this book you have managed to convince millions of Americans, people all over the world, really, that you are in fact the long-awaited second coming of Jesus Christ. Millions of people have been waiting to see what you look like, yet you've voluntarily stayed in a mental institution until your appearance here tonight. Why have you kept yourself out of sight until tonight? And why don't you look special, somehow, if you don't mind me asking?

JESUS:
I like you, Johnny. I wish everyone had the healthy attitude you have. I've kept out of sight because the real Jesus is only an idea, not a person. I'm a person. That screws up everything.

The real Jesus was manufactured by politicians. The actual Jesus got lost in the dust 2000 years ago. The real Jesus is the only Jesus left, but it's not the actual Jesus. I am the actual Jesus, as my book makes clear.

But now I'm ready to kick some ass. I wouldn't be able to kick any ass if I were simply Arnold Mansfield. So I had to become Jesus. Which is simply a matter of belief. Without

39

believers, there is no Jesus.

And I never intended that people make some kind of God out of me. My book doesn't address that point. But I had to get the attention of the people, which is why I wrote the book the way I did.

JOHNNY:
So what is this? You're Jesus, yet you're not? I mean, if I had a Jesus gig going, I'd think twice about giving it up. [Laughs.]

JESUS:
I heard that! There's been a real temptation to simply go for it. Jesus is a hell of a lot bigger business today than it was 2000 years ago, believe me. But there's greed on the one hand, and there's the best interests of people on the other. I love people, even if they are such assholes.

JOHNNY:
[To EDDIE.] Can we say that on the air?

EDDIE:
[Leans toward off stage, as if listening for an answer.] The producer says that Jesus can say anything he damn well pleases.

JESUS:
Then, as I was saying, people are such assholes. I have immense concern and pity for them. And that overwhelms any temptation I may have for capitalizing on the Jesus business.

JOHNNY:
What is this business about your book having healing power? What's happening there? Is that for real?

40

JESUS:

The basic principle behind any reality, in this case the reality of sickness, is that it is the product of personal creativity. If people were in better tune with themselves, they would see that they create their own sicknesses and diseases, and that such things can be uncreated very simply. The natural state of the body is good health. But a sick mind, that is, a mind that is out of touch with the inner or higher self, makes many mistakes. However, no such mistake is permanent. We live in an environment of perpetual creativity, where nothing can even continue without being constantly recreated.

So the opportunity to recreate in a different fashion, say, to change sickness to health, is ever-present. The book, of course, has nothing to do with it. It's simply a way of focusing creative energy.

JOHNNY:

I wish I understood what you just said. It sounded important.

CREWMAN FOUR:

[Signals break.]

JOHNNY:

We have to break now for this message. Hear ye the word of the sponsor. [Laughs.] We'll be right back.

[Two minutes pass with nothing much happening on stage. Johnny and Jesus converse, but the audience can barely hear them. Commercials roll on the monitor.]

CREWMAN FOUR:
Fifteen seconds! Ten, nine, eight, seven, six, five, four, three.

Scene 7, The Second Jesus Scene

JOHNNY:
We were just talking during the break. Tell me again how you got around the fact that your second coming took place in a mental institution. After all, everyone was expecting you to come down out of the clouds, and you really took a wrong left turn there somewhere! [Laughs.]

JESUS:
Simple, really. If people are willing to believe that a man can come flying out of the clouds without a parachute, it's not hard to get them to believe that a man can come out of a mental institution. Technically, by travelling over the air waves, I am coming out of the clouds right now, by way of television.

JOHNNY:
You said a man. Aren't you some kind of a god or something? I mean, there's been a lot of talk. [Laughs.]

JESUS:
What you see is what you get. No, that God business happened after I left the scene. Assholes, again, got everything screwed up, mostly for reasons of power. I never said I was a God.

JOHNNY:
What about "I and my Father are one?"

JESUS:
Everyone and his Father are one. They are one. That's a mystery because people don't understand Father. Father is a higher aspect of oneself, it's not somebody else. People, for the most part, have no contact with this higher self, and when they do sometimes contact it, they usually don't realize it's only a part of themselves.

JOHNNY:
Looks like we're getting into some heavy, uh, mud here. [Laughs.] So. See if I've got this straight. If Father is self, then am I my own grandfather? [Laughs.] No, I mean, where does God fit in?

JESUS:
In most senses that the word is understood, there is no God.

JOHNNY:
[Genuinely shocked.] Oh, my God. [Covers his face with his hands.] Do you say this in your book? I haven't read your book, by the way. I just, I don't know, I couldn't get myself to somehow.

JESUS:
Interesting point there, Johnny. Very few people have read it. Reviewers, mostly, and a few brave souls. It's been talked about a great deal and has sold terrifically. But people are so guilt-ridden these days that they can't face the confrontation of actually reading it. Similar to another best seller.

JOHNNY:
The Bible?

JESUS:
So the stories that are going around about me and the book
are based on old beliefs, with a few expedient revisions that
have come in handy. Isn't it amazing how many books
people will read concerning their hobbies, and how few that
relate to their life and death? Assholes.

JOHNNY:
That's a good point. I suppose I've read every golf book
ever written. But I did read the Bible once, when I was a
kid. Cover to cover. [AUDIENCE EXTRAS applaud.]
Well, I ran out of Zane Grey books. [Laughs.]
Oh, I know what I want to ask you. Miracles-how do you
do miracles. Is it something that you could, say, teach me to
do?

JESUS:
Most of the miracles attributed to me in the New Testament
never happened. They were creative writing projects that
coincided with the desire of politicians to make me a God.
But there is such a thing as real magic, by which I mean the
application of certain little-known natural laws. I
demonstrated some of that magic, and those incidents, like
the healings, provided the basis for all the other miracle
stories, starting with the virgin birth. May-December
couplings and illegitimacy are not modern inventions, you
know.

JOHNNY:
Okay. When did you decide to become Jesus, or discover
that you are, as the case may be?

JESUS:
Oh, some ten years ago. You see, I read a book called The
True Believer by Eric Hoffer, and it showed me how I

could convince millions of people that I am Jesus. So I did it.

JOHNNY:
Well, how about it, then? Are you really Jesus, or just somebody who decided to give it a try? Run it up the flagpole and see who shouts Hosanna? [Laughs.]

JESUS:
Both. I am Jesus, because people believe in me. They're completely convinced of it, as you well know. And that's what Jesus is, a belief in the minds of people. So that's me. Even the original Jesus decided one day to become Jesus. Before that, he was just another crazy.
Crazies mostly ran around loose in those days, you know.

JOHNNY:
So there's no actual relationship between you and the historical Jesus.

JESUS:
Oh, not true. I have a complete memory of that lifetime. A lot of it came to me during my childhood, but it frightened me because it didn't fit into today's reality, and I managed to end up in a mental institution. Later in life, I found techniques that enabled me to remember more and more, and to deal with it as an adult.

JOHNNY:
How do you know it's not just your imagination?

JESUS:
How do you know that your memory of yesterday is not your imagination? It's an unanswerable question, because memory and imagination are so closely intertwined. We can't recall memories without using imagination to do so.

JOHNNY:
If you say so. I've never thought about that. But that's interesting about you remembering the life of Jesus. Sort of like reincarnation or something, isn't it?

JESUS:
Sort of. Like most beliefs, reincarnation reflects an element of truth. We do live many lives, but we do it all at once, not one after another. You see, time is another belief that contains only an element of truth.

CREWMAN FOUR:
[Signals break.]

JOHNNY:
You're calling time a belief? Well, I believe it's time for a few messages from the folks who pay the bills. [Laughs.] We'll be right back with more from Jesus Christ. No, wait...is it time? Yes, we'll be back with a special performance by the Mile-High Players.

[Stage empties. JOHNNY and JESUS get dressed for skits. CREWMEN and STAGE HANDS install a painted backdrop of a street of shops in front of background curtain. They ad lib, swearing at each other a lot. Two minutes pass. JOHNNY and JESUS take their positions, one on each side of the backdrop.]

Scene 8. The Mile-High Players

EDDIE:
[Standing in front of backdrop.] You may not have asked for it, but you've got it. The Johnny Show presents...The Mile-High Players!

JOHNNY:
[Enters from stage right, dressed in white robe, wearing long white hair and white beard, carrying placard on stick that reads "Siners Repentt." He parades back and forth once, shouting:] Repent! The end of the world is at hand! Sinners, repent! [Exits stage right.]

JESUS:
[Enters stage left, same appearance as JOHNNY, his placard reads "End of Wurld at Hande." He shouts:] Repent your sins! The end of the world is coming! Sinners repent! [Exits stage left.]

JOHNNY and JESUS:
[Each enters same as before, not seeing each other. In unison they shout:] The end of the world is at hand! [Startled, they turn to look at each other, crouch, and in unison ask each other:] When??

JOHNNY:
I see we go to the same sign painter.

JESUS:
[Looks at placards, lets out an exaggerated moan, drapes an arm over Johnny's shoulder, and sings:] Nobody knows the trouble I've seen, nobody knows but Jesus.

JOHNNY:
So, how's business?

JESUS:
Ain't worth a shit. How about you?

JOHNNY:
Not too good. I'm thinking of getting a new routine.

JESUS:
Good idea! What do you have in mind?

JOHNNY:
I was thinking that I should do something with more popular appeal.

JESUS:
Good thinking! This end of the world business is just about used up. Every day the same thing, and does the world end? No, it's just another day, another dollar.

JOHNNY:
You make that much? A one-figure income?

JESUS:
Figure of speech. So what would be more popular?

JOHNNY:
My idea is to take requests. Whatever people want me to holler, I'll holler. I don't see how it can miss.

JESUS:
Wonderful! But what will you put on your sign?

JOHNNY:
I've already thought about that. [Turns sign around; it reads "This Space Fer Rent"]

JESUS:
Sounds too good to pass up. [He makes a magical zap motion at his placard, turns it around, and it reads "This Space Four Rent"]

JOHNNY:
You mean, you're going to steal my idea, just like that?

JESUS:
And I suppose you invented the end of the world?

JOHNNY:
Okay, okay. Say, here come a couple of people now. Let's give it a try. [Shouting:] Hollering for rent!

JESUS:
[Shouting:] Custom hollering at your request!

COUPLE:
[They enter as if passing by, but stop.]

JOHNNY:
[After glaring at Jesus.] Trained professional voice will holler your message!

JESUS:
[Laughing.] Voice of God here!

MAN:
Say, how does this work?

JOHNNY:
You tell me what you want me to holler and I holler it.
Cheap rates.

JESUS:
I have a better voice, and lower rates.

WOMAN:
Gee, Ray, what do you think? Do we need some?

MAN:
Couldn't hurt, I guess. What holler should we order?

WOMAN:
How about, "I love Ray."

MAN:
And, "I love Jenny."

JESUS:
I'll take the "I love Jenny."

JOHNNY:
[Glaring at Jesus.] If you think I'm going to stand out here
and holler "I love Ray," you're crazy!

MAN:
[To JESUS.] How much will that be?

JESUS:
I think a fiver will cover it.

MAN:
[Hands five dollars to JESUS, turns to Johnny with another fiver in his hand.] How much for you?

JOHNNY:
[Eyes the fiver in Jesus' hand, then the one in Ray's hand, rubs his stomach as if hungry.] It'll take more than five.

MAN:
I understand. How about twenty?

JOHNNY:
You've got a deal. [Accepts the twenty.]

COUPLE:
[They stand to the side and listen.]

JESUS:
I love Jenny!

JOHNNY:
Twenty bucks says I love Ray!

[Applause sign lights up. JOHNNY and JESUS exit. EDDIE takes position in front of backdrop.]

EDDIE:
We'll be right back with more from Jesus Christ, so don't go away!

[Two minutes pass, during which the street scene backdrop is removed. Nothing much else seems to happen. Commercials roll on the monitor. JOHNNY and JESUS get out of costume and appear on stage when CREWMAN FOUR announces nine seconds. They dash for their seats.]

53

CREWMAN FOUR:
Fifteen seconds! Ten, nine, eight, seven, six, five, four, three.

Scene 9, The Third Jesus Scene

JOHNNY:
We're back with more of Jesus Christ. Jesus, one thing has been nagging at me. You...you swear. I didn't expect that.

JESUS:
I'm a common man, Johnny, born lower class, just as I was 2000 years ago. When I kicked the money-changers out of the temple, do you imagine I went in there saying, "Now you naughty boys had better leave?" I told them to haul ass. I speak the language of my people. This business of swearing being a sin is just another example of how corrupted my original teachings have become. The only thing I ever said in that regard was that people shouldn't take oaths in God's name. The reason for that is that it reinforces the idea that God is somehow separate from us, and I fought that idea as much as I could.

You are the temple of God, I said, He is within you. But no. For that matter, this whole idea of sin is sick. There's no such thing as sin. There are only more or less desirable states of being.

JOHNNY:
[Swearing.] Well, Jesus Christ, I guess that clears that up. It feels funny to say Jesus Christ and realize that it's someone's name.

JESUS:

It's not, of course. It's the name that was given to me by the church.

JOHNNY:
That's right. Christ means, uh, it means something, doesn't it? What does it mean?

JESUS:
I'm not a theologian. Jesus Christ, give me a break, will you? I'm just a teacher of natural things.

JOHNNY:
Hey, no big deal, Jesus. I'll look it up. Let's talk about your teachings. Basically, what...love your neighbor?

JESUS:
What I taught was that all men should discover how to love themselves, and having accomplished that, they would find that they love all men, for they would know what a man is. Women too, of course. I was the original women's rights advocate.

JOHNNY:
What about this born-again business that has come about recently? Salvation. How has that teaching survived the ages?

JESUS:
About as well as you'd expect--lousy. What I taught is that man is a much greater being than he realizes, that great power is within him, a power I called the Father, although it's part of oneself, and that it can be experienced if you turn your sight inward, away from the outside world. Not permanently, just a little while each day, like eating.
To ignore this possibility is a great loss, a tragedy, really. I used the word hell to give my contention some weight, and

described the wonders of exploring inside oneself as heaven, although these have come to be thought of as places, which is just so much perverted bullshit.

JOHNNY:
Well, folks, I tried to stall off the sermon as long as I could. [Laughs.] No, really, I'm glad to hear you say that. I've never had a good opinion of hell or heaven, either one. Hell is a dirty trick, and heaven always sounded boring to me. But how did we get this born-again phenomenon out of that?

JESUS:
More politics. Hell became a weapon of fear, and the political leaders expanded on it to give themselves power over people. Then, having created a terrible problem, they created the solution, with themselves holding a monopoly on it.

To think that a soul can be lost or condemned is utter nonsense. Even if it could, to think that some superficial rite of salvation, however emotional, could correct the situation is even greater lunacy.

JOHNNY:
These must be, ah, some of the things you wanted to get said on national TV, right?

JESUS:
It's ridiculous to see a major religion called Christianity. I managed to teach my methods of inner exploration, call it self-realization or enlightenment or whatever you want, to a total of twelve people.

Anybody could put my teachings to work for them, but the sad fact is that very few people actually ever have. I doubt if there have been as many as 500 who have done so in the past 2000 years. People, for the most part, are lazy assholes who'd rather believe the perversions of some preacher than do a little thinking and reading of their own. It's all in my book. And that's all I have to say, Johnny, so... [Gets up to leave.] It's been a slice! [Shakes JOHNNY's hand and exits.]

Scene 10, Billy Bob

JOHNNY:
[Recovering from Jesus' abrupt departure.] Jesus Christ, folks! [Applause sign lights up.] I guess he just ran out of material. [Laughs.] I suppose I could loan him a few of my writers. Not that they write any good stuff, but they produce so much of it!

I do have another guest waiting in the wings. That's called contingency planning. We invited the Pope, but he wouldn't take the spot on a standby basis. The Pope never has commented publicly on this Jesus, has he? No, I don't think so. Anyway, the Pope declined. Really, we invited him.

CREWMAN FOUR :
[Signals break.]

JOHNNY :
Dear Your Reverend Holy Father, the whole treatment. In fact, we had a devil...make that a dickens of a time getting someone to appear after Jesus tonight, in case the show ran short. I guess it's a hot seat once Jesus has been in it. Anyway, we'll be right back with...the Reverend Billy Bob Jackson from Odessa, Texas. Billy Bob Jackson!

[Applause sign lights up. Commercials roll during two minute break. JOHNNY walks around the stage, talking to STAGE MANAGER, EDDIE and others, adjusting to the abrupt shift in the show.

JOHNNY :
[Returns to his seat.] We're back, and lets give a big hand to the Reverend Billy Bob Jackson from Odessa, Texas!

BILLY BOB :
[Takes guest seat on sofa and begins talking as soon as applause dies down.] Johnny, the Bible says that in the last days there will be false prophets, and I confess before America tonight that I was just as gullible as the rest of the fine, wonderful people of our great country in thinking that this imposter was the second coming of our Lord.
May God forgive me. As I sat backstage and listened to this man curse and blaspheme in the name of our Savior, I felt my insides turning in disgust, as I'm sure every God-fearing Christian did. Foul language fit only for the gutter from the mouth of our Lord? Monstrous! I just praise God that he didn't get on the subject of sex!

JOHNNY :
I wonder, Billy Bob, if you could make your position just a little more clear? [Laughs.] So you no longer believe that this man is Jesus? I don't know, he made a lot of sense to me. What he said...

BILLY BOB :
[Interrupting.] No matter what he said. Just think of how he said it. Gutter-mouth sinner. The man is bound for the fires of hell, mark my words.

JOHNNY :
Well, nobody can say we aren't presenting both sides of the issue. [Laughs.] Billy Bob, did you even hear what he said?

BILLY BOB :
No, sir! I tuned the man out so I wouldn't offend my ears with the foul sounds of his garbage mouth. It's disgraceful,

Johnny. I certainly pray that no children were awake to hear this filth invading the sanctity of their homes.

JOHNNY :
Billy Bob, the way he put it, he said he was a common man, a man of the people, and he spoke their language. That makes sense to me.

BILLY BOB :
Everybody knows that foul language is a sin.

JOHNNY :
Does it say so in the Bible?

BILLY BOB :
The Bible plainly says not to take God's name in vain, nor to swear any oath in God's name. Isn't that clear enough? Nor swear any oath!

JOHNNY :
What is it they do in court when they swear in a witness? That's swearing an oath and it ends up with the words, "So help me God." Are you saying that our court system is operating against the Bible?

BILLY BOB :
That's not what the Bible means. Sure, the word is the same, but you need the guidance of the Holy Spirit to help you decide which meaning of the word is intended. God has spoken very clearly on the issue, and foul language is clearly a sin.

JOHNNY :
Does the Holy Spirit talk to you, Billy Bob?

BILLY BOB :
Johnny, I'm only a country preacher, but even to the likes
of me the voice of the Holy Spirit is heard.

JOHNNY :
What does it sound like? Does it have a Jewish accent?
[Laughs.]

BILLY BOB :
The Holy Spirit does not speak in words.

JOHNNY :
Then how do you know what it's saying?

BILLY BOB :
It's more like it takes over your mind and gives you its
thoughts.

JOHNNY :
It takes over your mind? How do you distinguish that from
certain types of mental illness?

BILLY BOB :
I don't think that you are seriously trying to understand.
Here I thought I had a chance to bring the word of the Lord
to the great Johnny, and you are sitting there making a
mockery of the gospel.

JOHNNY :
Oh, no. I'm not mocking the gospel. I'm quite serious about
my question. I mean, if anything else took over your
thoughts, you'd be called insane. How do you know the
difference with the Holy Spirit?

BILLY BOB :
Because the Holy Spirit comes to you in the sanctity of

prayer, that's how.

JOHNNY :
Does it ever happen that the Holy Spirit says different
things to different people?

BILLY BOB :
How could that possibly happen?

JOHNNY :
I'm just guessing, but I would think that the Holy Spirit has
told many people that my guest tonight was really Jesus
Christ. Would you say that that's probably true? [BILLY
BOB does not answer.]

I mean, surely people asked the Holy Spirit to check this
guy out, and there couldn't have been many negative
reports, judging from the number of people who have
accepted him as Jesus, sight unseen.

Did you check with the Holy Spirit before you decided that
this man really is Jesus? And did you check with the Holy
Spirit before changing your mind about him? I know this is
kind of a hectic place for praying, but maybe that's what
you were doing backstage, I don't know.

CREWMAN FOUR
[Signals break.]

BILLY BOB :
[Has become very agitated.] I...Johnny, this place...the
Holy Spirit...if this man really is Jesus...oh, my God, what
am I going to do? Oh, shit! I mean,.. oh, shit! [Runs from
stage.]

JOHNNY :
Sorry I had to do that, but we're out of time. [Flips a pencil over his shoulder.] From Odessa, Texas...Billy Bob Jackson! [Applause sign lights up.] Good night, folks!

[CREWMEN and STAGE HANDS amble onto stage and begin reversing the props and setup procedure that opened the show. Cast credits appear on the monitor. There is much ad libbing and swearing. There is no signal for the audience to leave except that, after a moment, AUDIENCE EXTRAS get up and leave.]

www.ingramcontent.com/pod-product-compliance
Lightning Source LLC
LaVergne TN
LVHW041208080426
835508LV00008B/858